CHRISTA McAULIFFE

Pioneer Space Teacher

Charlene W. Billings

ENSLOW PUBLISHERS, INC.

Bloy St. & Ramsey Ave.   P.O. Box 38
Box 777   Aldershot
Hillside, N.J. 07205   Hants GU12 6BP
U.S.A.   U.K.

Library of Congress Cataloging in Publication Data

Billings, Charlene W.
  Christa McAuliffe: pioneer space teacher.

  Includes index.
  Summary: Describes the "life before stardom" and selection of a New Hampshire teacher as the first private citizen to go into space, her training as an astronaut, and the shuttlecraft disaster that ended her life.
  1. McAuliffe, Christa, 1948-1986—Juvenile literature. 2. Astronauts—United States—Biography—Juvenile literature. 3. Teachers—New Hampshire—Biography—Juvenile literature. 4. Challenger (Spacecraft)—Juvenile literature. [1. McAuliffe, Christa, 1948-1986. 2. Astronauts. 3. Teachers. 4. Challenger (Spacecraft)] 1. Title.
TL789.85.M33B55 1986 629.45'0092'4 [B] [92] 86-13453
ISBN 0-89490-148-6

Printed in the United States of America

10 9 8 7 6 5

Illustration Credits
Carlyjane's Studio, p. 62; Courtesy of Marian High School, pp. 18, 19, 20, 45; NASA, pp. 13, 14, 26, 28, 32, 34, 36, 41, 42, 49, 51, 60; Wide World Photos, pp. 9, 53.

For Christa McAuliffe and the courageous crew of *Challenger*

Acknowledgments

I extend my sincere appreciation to the employees at the Johnson Space Center, the Kennedy Space Center, and NASA headquarters in Washington, D.C., for providing information and photographs for this book. Thank you also to Joyce Cavanaugh, Director of Development, Marian High School, Framingham, Massachusetts, and to Charles F. Foley, Principal, Concord High School, Concord, New Hampshire, for their thoughtful cooperation and permission to use school and year-book photographs. Special thanks go to Kathy Richardson of the Nashua Public Library Children's Room, who put the publisher and me in touch with each other, and to those who encouraged me after the terrible events of January 28, 1986.

Contents

Preface

In August 1985 I began research for a biography about Christa McAuliffe. Enslow Publishers had sought a New Hampshire author to write a book for young people about the teacher who would go into space. When school began in September 1985, teacher Christa McAuliffe went to Johnson Space Center to prepare to ride the space shuttle *Challenger* into history, and I began to write her biography.

The book would tell the story of an exceptional teacher, one who was willing to take risks to achieve her goals. She wanted to encourage America's schoolchildren to take more interest in the space program. At the same time, she wanted to increase respect for the teaching profession. In preparation for the flight, she practiced lessons that would be broadcast live from space to classrooms across the country. A space age journal she planned to write would describe what travel was like for a pioneer at the frontier of space.

On January 28, 1986, the worst disaster in the history of space flight took place. The space shuttle *Challenger* blew up only seventy-four seconds into its flight. Christa McAuliffe and her fellow astronauts were killed. The entire nation mourned the seven American space heroes. The tragedy brought a more profound meaning to writing this biography than either I or the publisher ever could have anticipated.

1

Teacher With the Right Stuff

News reporters and photographers crowded the Roosevelt Room at the White House. It was July 19, 1985, and a sense of excitement filled the air. For over ten months, the National Aeronautics and Space Administration (NASA) had been searching to find America's first private citizen passenger to go into space. As a tribute to the teaching profession, President Ronald Reagan had promised that a schoolteacher would be selected for this special mission.

More than ten thousand hopeful teachers from all over the United States and its territories had applied. Now only ten finalists remained. Rumors and predictions had been heard around Washington, D.C., for days—but the secret of who had been chosen had been carefully guarded until the last moment.

The ten finalists entered the Roosevelt Room as a group. Vice-President George Bush stepped forward and spoke.

We're here today to announce the first private citizen in the history of space flight. . . . NASA, with the help of the heads of our state school systems, has searched the nation for a teacher with the right stuff. Really, there are thousands, thousands of teachers with the right stuff. . . . We are honoring all those teachers of merit today, and we're doing something else, because . . . the more than a hundred semifinalists will all, in the months ahead, serve . . . as a link between NASA and the nation's school system. These teachers have all received special NASA training to pass on to the other teachers and to their students.

So let me tell you now who our teacher in space will be. . . . I thought I was a world traveler, but this tops anything I've tried.

First Vice-President Bush named the runner-up. Barbara Morgan, a second-grade teacher from McCall, Idaho, would train as the alternate to ride the space shuttle into orbit.

Then came the moment everyone was awaiting. Christa McAuliffe, a social studies teacher from Concord, New Hampshire, was proclaimed the winner! She and Vice-President Bush smiled joyfully as he congratulated her and they shook hands.

Christa McAuliffe was given an Oscar-sized trophy of a student looking up to a teacher, who was pointing at the stars. From then on, Christa McAuliffe, the teacher who was to go into space, would *be* a star!

What would Christa say after receiving this great honor? She had only moments to consider her thoughts:

It's not often that a teacher is at a loss for words. I know my students wouldn't think so.

I've made nine wonderful friends over the last two

weeks. And when that shuttle goes, there might be one body but there are going to be ten souls that I'm taking with me.

Thank you.

Teacher Christa McAuliffe is congratulated by Vice-President George Bush at the White House after he announced she would be the first private citizen to go into space. Looking on is Peggy Lathlaen, a teacher from Friendswood, Texas.

For two weeks Christa and the nine other teachers who were finalists had been competing with each other. But now the other teachers hugged and congratulated Christa. They knew she was an outstanding choice. And they knew, too, that Christa McAuliffe would represent them and other dedicated teachers everywhere well.

Later, at a news conference on the north lawn of the White House, Christa was asked why she thought she had been NASA's first choice. She replied, "I don't know. I thought they would have to put everybody's name in a hat to pick a winner." How did it feel to be chosen? "I'm still kind of floating. I don't know when I'll come down to earth," she said.

How had Christa McAuliffe been selected from so many worthy candidates? How had NASA found the best teacher for this exciting mission?

In November 1984 an "Announcement of Opportunity" was distributed nationwide by NASA. It described how the teacher in space would be chosen, listed the medical requirements, and explained the responsibilities of the teacher who would be selected. Teachers could apply from December 1, 1984, to February 1, 1985.

Without hesitation, Christa McAuliffe decided to apply. She had been excited about space exploration from its very beginnings in the late 1950s when the first artificial satellites were launched into orbit. Her father recalls that when she told him about her application, she said, "Dad, I'm going."

On her application to the NASA Teacher in Space Project, Christa McAuliffe was asked: "Why do you want to be the first U.S. private citizen in space?" She answered:

> I remember the excitement in my home when the first satellites were launched. My parents were amazed and I was caught up with their wonder. In school, my classes would gather around the TV and try to follow the rocket as it seemed to jump all over the screen. I remember when Alan Shepard made his historic flight—not even an orbit— and I was thrilled. John Kennedy inspired me with his words about placing a man on the moon and I still

remember a cloudy, rainy night driving through Pennsylvania and hearing the news that the astronauts had landed safely.

As a woman, I have been envious of those men who could participate in the space program. and who were encouraged to excel in the areas of math and science. I felt that women had indeed been left outside of one of the most exciting careers available. When Sally Ride and other women began to train as astronauts, I could look among my students and see ahead of them an ever-increasing list of opportunities.

I cannot join the space program and restart my life as an astronaut, but this opportunity to connect my abilities as an educator with my interests in history and space is a unique opportunity to fulfill my early fantasies. I watched the Space Age being born and I would like to participate.

The competition wasn't to be easy for Christa. Teachers responded from all of the fifty states, the District of Columbia, Puerto Rico, Guam, the Virgin Islands, overseas U.S. schools, and Bureau of Indian Affairs schools. From over ten thousand applications state, territorial, and NASA review panels selected two semifinalists from each state and U.S. territory. With this process, the review panels narrowed the field of teachers to 114 candidates. Christa survived the first cut.

The next hurdle was a meeting of the 114 nominees in Washington, D.C., from June 22 to June 27, 1985. During this time, a National Review Panel of distinguished people selected the ten finalists in the competition. The National Review Panel included three former astronauts, a former U.S. commissioner of education, three college presidents and administrators, a former state governor, a former U.S. congresswoman, four educators, a former NASA official, a former professional basketball player, two business executives, two professional actors, and a physicist. Again Christa succeeded. She became one of the ten finalists.

The final step for the ten teachers remaining in the competition was to be tested and interviewed further by the NASA Space Flight Participant Evaluation Committee. The ten finalists went to Johnson Space Center in Houston, Texas, on July 7, 1985. Over the next several days they had complete medical examinations, physical and psychological fitness tests, and briefings about space flight.

For the physical fitness tests, each candidate ran on a treadmill while wired to instruments that monitored breathing, blood pressure, and other body responses. The teachers each measured their strength on a space-age muscle-building machine. Physicians examining them seemed to poke and prod every muscle and organ of their bodies.

One of the psychological tests required each teacher to spend ten minutes curled up inside a fabric ball, only thirty-four inches in diameter, that was zipped shut from the outside. This was to learn if any of the teachers were bothered by claustrophobia, the fear of being in an enclosed or confined place. Christa rated this as her most difficult experience.

The candidates also had to answer written psychological questions such as this one:

> What kind of animal do your friends see you as?
> (a) fox, (b) beaver, (c) cat, (d) puppy, (e) owl, (f) lion.

Christa answered (b) and (c) because she was often busy as a beaver and was independent, like a cat.

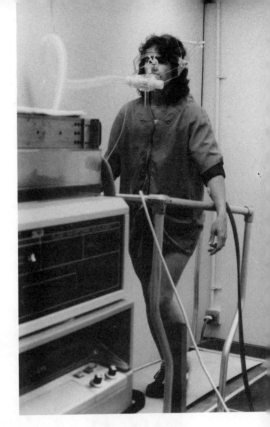

Christa undergoes a physical fitness test on a treadmill at Johnson Space Center in Houston, Texas.

One day, after hours of instruction about space flight, the finalists entered an altitude test chamber. This special "room" simulates sudden drastic changes in altitude. Christa and the other finalists were told they must learn to recognize the symptoms of lack of oxygen within their bodies. When symptoms appeared they must get oxygen immediately.

As the chamber simulated conditions at altitudes of up to thirty-five thousand feet, some teachers' fingers turned blue. They had to breathe oxygen from gas masks. When Christa had difficulty breathing and her vision became blurry, she realized that she needed to use her oxygen mask.

In addition, all of the candidates flew in a specially outfitted NASA KC-135 airplane that has been nicknamed the "Vomit

Comet." This was a test to see whether any of the teachers would be likely to feel sick to their stomachs in the weightlessness of space. Christa had some concern about this because she had had motion sickness as a youngster. But she gamely climbed aboard the plane.

The KC-135 repeatedly flew them in roller-coaster-like loops. For a few moments during each loop the teachers floated in the air, experiencing weightlessness similiar to what they would feel all the time if they were traveling in space. Christa passed this and all the other tests with flying colors.

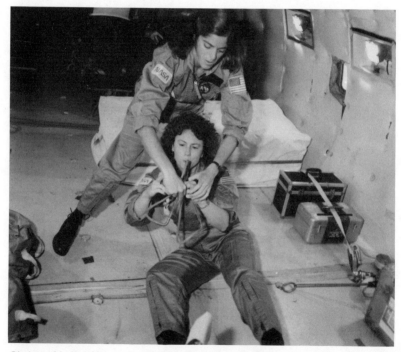

Christa McAuliffe and Barbara Morgan conduct a motion test under weightless conditions. All of the finalists in the Teacher in Space Project experienced weightlessness in a special NASA KC-135 training jet before Christa was selected as the primary candidate.

The top ten teachers returned to Washington, D.C., for final interviews. The results of their tests and interviews were judged by a panel of seven senior NASA officials who recommended a primary candidate and a runner-up for the Teacher in Space Project to James M. Beggs, chief administrator of NASA. Both the winner and the runner-up would undergo the training necessary to prepare for the space shuttle Mission 51-L. If the primary candidate could not fly, the runner-up would go into orbit instead.

The final review panel of seven senior NASA officials unanimously selected Christa McAuliffe as their first choice. Though they all agreed it was a very difficult job, they reached their decision in less than one hour. Ann Bradley, chairwoman of the panel, said of McAuliffe, "To her credit, she did everything right."

Late in the day on July 19 Christa McAuliffe flew from Washington, D.C., back to meet her family in New Hampshire. Despite the lateness of her arrival, news reporters, a large crowd of well-wishers, and bagpipe music greeted her that night at the airport.

How did other people feel about Christa's sudden fame? Right after her selection, her husband of fifteen years, Steven McAuliffe, said, "There may have been candidates of her equal, but none superior to her. She was selected because she is unpretentious and a genuinely nice person whom people really identify with." Steven McAuliffe thought of his wife as a "pioneer" and believed she would dramatically increase public respect for the teaching profession.

Christa's parents were thrilled that their daughter had been chosen as the teacher to go into space. Her mother, Grace

Corrigan, said that Christa had always been "interested in everything." And her father, Edward Corrigan, thought she would be a "wonderful representative for NASA."

The next day Christa was cheered by thousands of citizens as she rode in an open convertible in a parade down the main street of Concord.

Further celebration was delayed while Christa traveled to appear on several television shows. When she returned to the capital city, the mayor proclaimed August 6, 1985, "Christa McAuliffe Day" with festivities held in the State House plaza. On that day Christa received commendations from the state and city, signed autographs for well-wishers, and led the band in a rousing rendition of "Stars and Stripes Forever." She said she was amazed at the excitement her selection had created in New Hampshire. But she enjoyed the local support.

She was delighted, too, by the recognition she had received when she appeared before a national meeting of the National Education Association. She said, "It was really special being honored by my peers."

Teachers, students, and citizens throughout the country seemed to agree that Christa McAuliffe was indeed a teacher who could communicate well and inspire other people with her enthusiasm—a teacher with the "right stuff."

2

Life Before Stardom

Sharon Christa Corrigan was born September 2, 1948, in Boston, Massachusetts. She spent most of her youth in Framingham, Massachusetts, where her parents still live. Her father, Edward Corrigan, is a retired accountant. Her mother, Grace Corrigan, is a former substitute teacher. From an early age, the Corrigans preferred to call their daughter Christa.

As soon as she could move about, young Christa displayed an independent spirit. One day, when she was still a toddler, she rode her tricycle several blocks from home onto Columbia Road, a major thoroughfare into Boston. Her dog, Teddy, and a neighbor rescued her from the traffic.

Christa's family was a closely knit one. As she grew older, she helped look after her four younger brothers and sisters. She made sure that they had as much fun on trips and outings as she did.

Grace Corrigan has recalled that Christa was quick to learn and was well liked by other people. "She always took over any situation and she always acted older than her age," said Christa's mother.

At six Christa became a Brownie and began a long association with the Girl Scouts. She spent part of her summers at Camp Wabasso in Bradford, New Hampshire. In the winter she skied on mountain trails in New Hampshire. At seventeen she competed for a trip to the annual Girl Scout Roundup in Idaho. She went to lectures, took tests, pitched tents blindfolded, and gave emergency first aid to win a train ride to Idaho the following summer.

Christa attended Marian High School, a coeducational Catholic school. She enjoyed music, took piano lessons, and performed in high school musicals. She was an All-American player on the Marian High softball team. In addition, she met and dated Steven McAuliffe, who would later become her husband.

Sharon Christa Corrigan and Steven McAuliffe at the Marian High School senior prom in 1966.

In high school, Christa did not originally plan to become a teacher. Though she had played school when she was little—as do many children—she "never had a burning desire" to make teaching her career.

Entrance to Marian High School, Framingham, Massachusetts, as it appears now.

After high school graduation in 1966, Christa went to college for four years. Her father had urged her to go away to school. But Christa enrolled at nearby Framingham State College and lived at home to save money for her younger brothers' and sisters' educations.

During the 1960s Christa and many other students at campuses all over the country were motivated by idealism. They recalled President John F. Kennedy's words given years earlier in his inaugural address on January 20, 1961: "Ask not what your country can do for you; ask what you can do for your country." Her generation was "caught up in that Kennedy charisma," Christa said.

They asked themselves, "How can we change the world?" Many of them joined the Peace Corps and VISTA (Volunteers in Service to America). Both of these government organizations sent volunteers who gave their time and talent to assist people who had asked for help. Peace Corps volunteers were assigned to areas outside of the country, and VISTA volunteers worked in the United States.

Christa, like many of her fellow students, wanted to make a difference. She was inspired to work toward a social service career. She was a good student in college, majored in history, and twice made the dean's list. She was a member of the glee club for four years and captain of the debate team for two years. In 1970 Christa received her bachelor of arts degree from Framingham State College.

Sharon Christa Corrigan's graduation picture as it appeared in the 1966 Marian High School Yearbook.

Later that summer, on August 23, 1970, Christa married Steven James McAuliffe. They had been sweethearts since their Marian High School days. Their feelings for each other had lasted through the years while Steven had attended the Virginia Military Institute in Lexington, Virginia, and Christa went to Framingham State College.

After their marriage the newlyweds moved to Maryland, and Steven went to Georgetown University Law School. Christa began her teaching career in 1970 at Benjamin Foulois Junior High School in Morningside, Maryland. She taught eighth-grade American history. From 1971 to 1978 Christa taught at Thomas Johnson Junior High School in Lanham, Maryland. Here her courses included eighth-grade English and American history and ninth-grade civics.

After graduating from Georgetown, Steven worked as a defense attorney in the appellate division of the Army Judge Advocate General's Corps. By 1975 he was working as a law clerk for the private practice of Stennis Hoyer, the president of the Maryland state senate. Steven tried to influence Christa to also become a lawyer. But she said she loved teaching and would consider nothing else. Christa enrolled at Bowie State College in Bowie, Maryland. She earned her master's degree in education in 1978.

Stennis Hoyer recalled, "Christa . . . always demonstrated a desire to relate what is going on in the public sphere to students." And John Hagan, her vice-principal at Thomas Johnson Junior High School, said, "She was a great teacher, and she really and truly loved the kids."

During the years she was teaching and working toward her master's degree, Christa gave birth to a son. Scott was born on September 11, 1976.

The McAuliffes moved to Concord, New Hampshire, during the blizzard of 1978. Steven had been hired as an assistant attorney general for the state of New Hampshire. Christa remembered the good times she had had in New Hampshire during the years she was growing up. She wanted to raise her own family in that state. The following year, on August 24, 1979, their daughter Caroline was born.

By the fall of 1980 Christa was back to teaching part time. She worked at Rundlett Junior High School in Concord teaching seventh-grade English and eighth-grade history. In the 1981–82 school year Christa taught ninth-grade English at Bow Memorial School in Bow, New Hampshire. After 1982 she taught tenth, eleventh, and twelfth grades at Concord High School. Her classes included economics, law, American history, and a course she developed entitled "The American Women."

In all, Christa McAuliffe spent twelve years actively teaching. She estimated that she had taught over fifteen hundred students in her career. Christa was drawn to teaching by the idea that she could influence so many students and that she could pass on to them life values as well as knowledge.

As a social studies teacher, she stressed the role that everyday people play in historical events. "I've always been concerned that ordinary people have not been given their place in history," she said.

One classroom discussion about the Revolutionary War in her "American Women" course focused on the role of women in the war effort. While men fought battles at places like Bunker Hill and Trenton, their wives and mothers sewed clothing, harvested crops, and prepared food and other goods that they contributed to help win the war. Christa emphasized that the struggles on the home front as well as on the battlefield must be included in an account of the Revolutionary War.

Her methods of teaching included hands-on experience. Her students have recalled that she often asked them to participate in recreating a particular event or decade in American history, rather than just lecturing to them about it. In her class about law, the students spent about half their time in courtrooms. They visited police stations and prisons. They also served as jurors in mock trials. In the "American Women" course students were required to keep daily journals as part of their assigned work.

The keeping of daily journals was not a new idea for Christa. She had been doing it herself for years. She first learned of their value in a course on the American West taught by Professor A. Carolla Haglund at Framingham State College. She was struck by the diary of Susan McGaffin, a pioneer who set out on the Santa Fe Trail on her wedding day. Christa discovered that much of the social history of the United States is to be found in personal letters, diaries, and travel accounts. Later, when she applied to NASA to become the teacher in space, her idea for a project was to keep a diary of what it is like to be a space traveler. She said, "I would like to humanize the Space Age by giving the perspective of a non-astronaut. I think the students will look at that and see that an ordinary person is contributing to history. If they can make that connection, they are going to get excited about history and about the future."

Christa likened what she wanted to do to the journeys of "the women who pioneered the West in Conestoga wagons. They didn't have a camera; they described things in vivid detail, in word pictures. They were concerned with daily tasks and the interaction between people, with hopes and fears. Those diaries and journals are the richest part of the history of our westward expansion—without them, it would just be how many Indians were killed and the number of settlements started."

McAuliffe wanted her students to think of the earth as a global village. While looking forward to her shuttle ride into space she said, "One of the wonderful things as a historian in space is for me to see the earth with no boundaries, to see the Spaceship Earth as a whole people. That is one of the things I try to foster when I teach international relations."

Why is it important for a teacher to fly into space? McAuliffe answered that question on her application to the Teacher in Space Project. She said, "space is the future. If as teachers we don't prepare the students for the future, we're not doing our jobs. We have to include it." She added that she wanted to help people "see space as a frontier . . . to show there is a new way of living." She also wanted to communicate the message that "space is for everyone."

When Christa taught at Bow Memorial School, she became president of the Bow Teacher's Union. She felt strongly about the importance of good teachers in the classroom. Her efforts in office won a raise for the teachers in that town.

While she lived in Concord, New Hampshire, Christa was involved in many community activities. She taught Christian doctrine classes at her parish church, St. Peter's. She helped raise funds for the Concord YWCA and the expansion of the local hospital. She was a member of the Junior Service League. Her family hosted inner-city students who were taking part in a program called "A Better Chance." Christa also was a Girl Scout leader.

Christa McAuliffe hoped to inspire more students to follow her lead. She wanted them to consider careers as teachers dedicated to excellence in education.

3

Teacher in Training

The fall of 1985 was very different for Christa McAuliffe. For the first time in years she would not return to the classroom to teach. On September 6 she visited Concord High School to say good-bye to the students and faculty. Three days later she began training at the Johnson Space Center in Houston to be the teacher in space.

The program of training for a passenger on the space shuttle was 120 hours of hard work. For Christa, the most difficult part was being away from her family. She called home as often as she could to share experiences with her husband and children. In November Steven, Scott, and Caroline visited her in Houston and toured the Johnson Space Center. And in December she went home for the holidays.

Christa worried about her physical fitness and stamina. She feared she might fall off the treadmill or have some medical problem that could bar her from the mission. But Dr. Don Stewart, chief of flight medicine at the Johnson Space Center, said that most healthy people could probably ride the space shuttle. The medical requirements for a passenger were not as hard to meet as those for the commander or pilot. Medical conditions that might keep Christa grounded were cancer, hernia, vertigo (dizziness), active ulcers, tinnitus (ringing in the ears), infectious diseases, or chronic conditions such as diabetes or arthritis. She was free of all of these.

Christa had other concerns as well. She wondered how her fellow crew members would feel about a newcomer to the program. They had trained for years to ride the shuttle, and she was a rookie. At their first meeting, Francis "Dick" Scobee, the mission commander, reassured Christa. He said, "No matter what happens on this mission, it's going to be known as the teacher mission. We feel that's good, because people will remember what we do."

Commander Francis Scobee briefs Christa in a shuttle mock-up.

Commander Scobee, forty-six, was from Cle Elum, Washington. He had a degree in aerospace engineering from the University of Arizona. He had flown forty-five different kinds of aircraft, including the Caribou C-7, which he flew on combat missions in Viet Nam. He started to train as an astronaut in 1978. He had piloted the space shuttle *Challenger* in 1984 on a mission that successfully repaired the Solar Max satellite in orbit. This satellite is investigating solar flares and radiation from the sun.

There would be five other crew members. Pilot Michael J. Smith, forty, had been raised on a farm in Beaufort, North Carolina. He went to the U.S. Naval Academy in Annapolis, Maryland. Like Dick Scobee, he was an experienced pilot. He had flown more than thirty kinds of airplanes and had won many medals for his military service in Viet Nam. He was picked for the space program in 1980. This would be his first shuttle flight.

Judith Resnik, thirty-six, was from Akron, Ohio. She was an electrical engineer with a bachelor's degree from Carnegie-Mellon University and a Ph.D. degree from the University of Maryland. She was picked from more than eight thousand applicants for the space program and began training in March 1978. She had flown once before on the space shuttle, in 1984.

Ronald E. McNair, thirty-six, grew up in Lake City, South Carolina. He did his undergraduate studies at North Carolina Agricultural and Technical State University at Greensboro. Then he went on in school to complete a doctorate in physics from the Massachusetts Institute of Technology. In 1978 he joined the space program. On his first shuttle flight in 1984 he launched a multi-million-dollar communications satellite into orbit.

Ellison S. Onizuka, thirty-nine, was an aerospace engineer from Hawaii. He had undergraduate and graduate degrees from the University of Colorado. He had been a test pilot and flight engineer for the Air Force for eight years before joining the space program in 1978. He had flown a secret military mission on the shuttle in January of 1985.

Gregory B. Jarvis, forty-one, was born in Detroit, Michigan. He earned a bachelor's degree in electrical engineering from the State University of New York at Buffalo and a master's degree in engineering from Northeastern University in Boston. He was in the Air Force from 1969 to 1973. He worked for Hughes Aircraft Company designing satellites when he applied and was picked by NASA in 1984 to do a series of experiments on the shuttle.

Mission 51-L crew portrait. *Front row, left to right;* Michael J. Smith, Francis R. Scobee, and Ronald E. McNair. *Back row, left to right;* Ellison S. Onizuka, S. Christa McAuliffe, Gregory B. Jarvis, and Judith A. Resnik.

In the event that Christa McAuliffe could not fly on the space shuttle, Barbara Radding Morgan would substitute for her. Barbara trained alongside Christa in Houston and, by the time of launch, also was ready for the flight and lessons from space.

Barbara Radding was born on November 28, 1951, in Fresno, California. She attended Stanford University and graduated with a bachelor of arts degree in human biology in 1973. She earned a teaching certificate from the College of Notre Dame in Belmont, California, in 1974.

On June 10, 1978, Barbara married Clayton Michael Morgan, a novelist and U.S. Forest Service smoke jumper. They have no children.

When she became a member of the project, she had taught for over ten years. In order to go into the program she went on leave from her job as a second-grade teacher at McCall-Donnelly Elementary School in McCall, Idaho.

During Christa's shuttle flight, Barbara was to serve as a television commentator. She would describe details of the mission and give additional information about the lessons from space to viewers on a daily one-hour program known as "Mission Watch."

Following the space flight, Christa McAuliffe and Barbara Morgan planned to visit classrooms all over the United States. They wanted to share the excitement and knowledge they would have gained as participants in NASA's Teacher in Space Project. They wanted to encourage students to study mathematics and science. They wanted to prepare students for a future that will include space stations, space factories, space law, and people doing business in space.

The training began with hours of briefings. Christa was given piles of workbooks to read. There was so much to learn! What did the space shuttle look like inside and out? What were the objectives of Mission 51-L? The workbooks were filled with an array of information. They told Christa how to read flight data files, how to enter and exit the space shuttle, which of the thirteen hundred switches in the cockpit *not* to touch, how to operate the equipment in the galley, how to use the cameras that would be on board, and even how to use the space shuttle's toilet.

Challenger was the name of the spacecraft Christa McAuliffe would ride. It was one of four space shuttle orbiters in NASA's fleet. The others were named *Columbia, Discovery,* and *Atlantis.*

Like the other orbiters in the fleet, *Challenger* resembled a wide-body jet airliner. Measuring 122 feet long and 78 feet across the wingspan, it was about the size of a DC-9 airplane. But instead of space for 150 passengers, a sixty-foot-long cargo bay took up most of the room. The *Challenger* astronauts would live, eat, sleep, and work inside the crew module in the front section of the spacecraft, near the blunt nose. The crew module had three levels. The upper level was the flight deck, where commander Scobee, pilot Michael Smith, and mission specialists Judith Resnik and Ronald McNair would sit during launch. The front of the flight deck contained instrument panels, monitors, displays, and controls for flying the orbiter. The rear wall of the flight deck contained additional displays and controls to be used with the payloads, or cargoes, on the mission. One of the controls located here operated the mechanical manipulator arm that was mounted in the cargo bay of the orbiter.

In the floor of the flight deck was a hatch to the middeck. The middeck would be where payload specialists Christa McAuliffe and Gregory Jarvis and mission specialist Ellison Onizuka would sit during launch.

On the left wall of the middeck was a forty-inch circular hatch through which the crew could enter or exit the spacecraft. Also on the left wall was the galley, where food and beverages were stored. Opposite the galley were four sleeping compartments, three stacked horizontal to the floor like bunk beds and the fourth a vertical sleep restraint. In the near-zero gravity of space Christa and the other crew members would be able to sleep comfortably in any position.

At the front of the middeck was a wall of lockers to hold crew members' belongings.

At the back of the middeck was the personal hygiene area. The toilet had a seat belt and foot straps. A curtain could be pulled for privacy when it was in use. Instead of water, an air suction system removed wastes. There was no shower on *Challenger*. The crew would wash with wet-wipes or at a sink that had a bowl-shaped dome over it to prevent water or soap bubbles from floating into the crew's living quarters.

Below the middeck was the equipment bay. This area was used to store equipment and contained parts of the waste disposal and life-support systems.

In the midsection of *Challenger* was the cargo compartment. It was sixty feet long and fifteen feet in diameter. Two clamshell-type doors could be opened in orbit to expose the large cargo bay.

The most important payload *Challenger* would carry was the TDRS-2 (Tracking and Data Relay Satellite-2) communications satellite. It would spin out of the cargo bay into orbit on the first day of *Challenger*'s mission. A small rocket built into the

TDRS-2 satellite would boost it into an orbit 22,300 miles above the earth. At this distance, the satellite would be in a geo-synchronous orbit. It would travel in pace with the earth's rotation, taking twenty-four hours to complete each orbit. For this reason it would appear stationary, remaining over the same location on the globe.

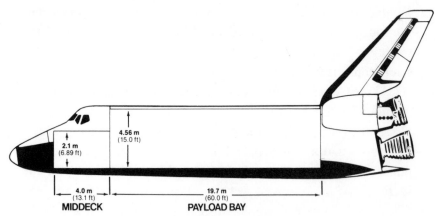

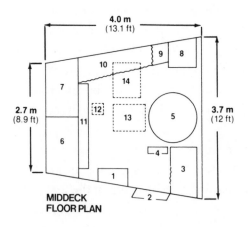

1 Galley	**7** Avionics bay 2	**Floor hatches**
2 Hatch	**8** Avionics bay 3	**12** Lithium h
3 Toilet	**9** Lockers	ide chan
4 Ladder to flight deck	**10** Sleep station	**13** Lithium h ide stora
5 Airlock	**11** Wall of lockers	**14** Wet trash storage
6 Avionics bay 1		

The TDRS-2 satellite would hover over Hawaii. It would team up with another similar satellite stationed over the coast of Brazil, the TDRS-1. The addition of TDRS-2 would enable NASA to be in touch with orbiters in space during all but a few minutes of each ninety-minute orbit. Without the TDRS-2, NASA would have to continue to rely on a system of ground bases dotted around the world to communicate with orbiters as they circle the earth at 17,500 miles per hour.

Another primary payload *Challenger* would have on board would be the Spartan-Halley carrier. This piece of equipment contained instruments designed to observe ultraviolet light from Comet Halley's tail. The Spartan-Halley carrier would be launched into orbit on the third day of the mission. On the fifth day, it would be retrieved from orbit using a fifty-foot mechanical arm mounted in *Challenger*'s cargo bay. It would be stowed in the cargo bay for return to earth.

At the back end of *Challenger* were its three main engines. When started at launch, each engine could produce 375,000 pounds of thrust. They were fueled from the huge, rust-colored external tank. Two smaller rocket engines at the back of *Challenger* each would provide about 6,000 pounds of thrust. They would give the spacecraft the final burst of speed it needed to go into orbit after the main engines shut down. They also would be used to maneuver the spacecraft while it was in orbit and to brake or slow down *Challenger* to start it on its return journey.

Small control engines located in the nose and rear end could change the attitude or position of the spaceship in orbit. Such maneuvers would be important when trying to retrieve the Spartan-Halley carrier from orbit, for example.

Challenger's wings were "double delta" wings. These were sharply swept backward and then flared out to a broader triangular shape. Along the edges of the wings were movable flaps called elevators and ailerons. The pilot could use these to dive, roll, or bank the craft during landing. The rudder, or tail, was for side-to-side stability.

Most of the outside of *Challenger* was covered with special, heat-resistant tiles. The tiles on the bottom of the orbiter could withstand temperatures up to 2,300°F. Along the leading edges of wings and on the nose, where the heat of reentry into the atmosphere would be most severe, were reinforced materials that could resist temperatures as high as 2,800°F.

Challenger could generate its own power from fuel cells that combined liquid hydrogen and oxygen. A by-product of this process was fresh water.

What would the atmosphere inside the crew module of *Challenger* be like for Christa and the other astronauts? It would be a mixture of about four parts of nitrogen and one part oxygen, much like the atmosphere here on earth. The crew quarters would be pressurized like the cabin of an airplane. A heat exchanger would keep the temperature inside the crew module as close to a spring day as possible—between 61°F. and 90°F. Excess heat produced by the crew and equipment in space would have to be removed, or it would become too hot to work inside the crew module within a few hours. The excess heat would be transferred to radiators mounted on the inside of the open doors of the cargo bay. From there it would radiate into space.

Challenger would not have enough power to go into space without the fuel stored in the large external tank and the two solid rocket boosters. The external fuel tank measured over 153 feet long and 27 feet in diameter. When fully loaded with liquid oxygen and liquid hydrogen, it would weigh over one and one-half million pounds. The fuel in the tank would flow through 17-inch-diameter fuel lines to *Challenger*'s main engines. In a normal launch, the giant external tank would be dropped after the fuel in it was completely used. It would break up when it hit the atmosphere more than fifty miles above the earth. The fuel tank would be the only part of the space shuttle that would not be reusable.

The twin solid rocket boosters on *Challenger* were 149 feet long and 12 feet in diameter. Filled with solid fuel, each one weighed well over one million pounds. During launch, the boosters would operate until they burned out, about 132 seconds. Then they would separate from the orbiter and float on parachutes into the sea. They would be recovered by ships, returned to land, and made ready for another space shuttle mission.

Christa was issued astronaut's clothing and a helmet. The clothing she received included such items as comfortable knit shirts, shorts, a T-shirt, underwear, socks, slippersocks, flight boots, gloves, and sky-blue pants, jacket, and coveralls. The pants had an adjustable waistband because in the near-zero gravity of space fluids rise from the lower body, changing a person's waist size. The jacket and coveralls had many zippered pockets. These would be necessary in the weightless conditions of space, where everything that is not secured can easily float away and be lost. An expert clothing technician at Johnson Space Center instructed Christa on how to use her helmet and visor during launch and reentry. He also showed her various supplies that she would carry for in-space activities. These included a watch, a small flashlight, pressurized pens, mechanical pencils, sunglasses, scissors, a pocketknife, and a sleep mask and earplugs.

NASA employee Alan Rochford assists McAuliffe with her helmet.

As part of her training, Christa had to learn how to zip herself into a sleep restraint. The restraint was much like a sleeping bag mounted on a firmly padded board. The bag would hold her snugly enough to make her feel as though she was lying on a comfortable bed. It would keep her from floating about and bumping into things as she slept in space. She could use her sleep mask and earplugs to block out light and sound.

A personal hygiene kit was given to Christa for the flight. It contained such items as nonfoaming toothpaste, a toothbrush, dental floss, soap, a hair comb and brush, skin lotion, and deodorant.

Christa was briefed about space photography. She was shown films taken from space. She became familiar with the motion picture camera that would be on board *Challenger.* She learned how to load and unload film magazines and how to adjust, install, and remove lenses. She practiced taking pictures with test subjects so that she would be able to take good, clear photographs from space.

The shuttle mission simulator was another important part of Christa's training. It could imitate the sensations of real space flight. In the simulator Christa experienced the surge of force she would feel during launch—a force three times as great as the gravity on earth. The windows of the simulator cockpit showed what someone sitting on the flight deck of the space shuttle orbiter would see during a real flight. The clearing of the tower at lift-off, the views of earth from space, and the fiery glow of the protective heat tiles during reentry appeared true-to-life. Sometimes lights flashed or alarms sounded to test Christa's and the crew's responses to an unexpected emergency.

Christa practiced two fifteen-minute lessons to be broadcast live from space to twenty-five million students in schools from

Florida to Alaska and Canada. In addition, several demonstrations done by Christa in space would be filmed for later viewing in the schools.

A special NASA KC-135 training jet was used to create brief periods of weightlessness. First the jet climbed steeply from twenty-six thousand to thirty-four thousand feet; then it went into a deep dive. For about thirty seconds at the top of the loop, Christa practiced in simulated weightlessness the lessons and demonstrations she would do in space. She said floating in midair made her feel just like Peter Pan.

The first lesson was called "The Ultimate Field Trip." Christa practiced giving a guided tour of the major areas of the shuttle orbiter and describing what was done in each area. The lesson began on the flight deck. Christa would introduce Commander Dick Scobee and Pilot Michael Smith. She then would show viewers *Challenger's* controls, computers, and cargo bay. After moving to middeck, Christa would point out the galley, sleeping quarters, and personal hygiene areas.

The second lesson had the title "Where We've Been, Where We're Going, Why?" At the beginning of this lesson Christa planned to tell viewers about the history and future of space flight using models of the Wright brothers' airplane and of the space station NASA has proposed to build in the 1990s. She would point out that only eighty-two years have passed between the first daring flight at Kitty Hawk, North Carolina, and our modern adventures in space.

Christa would describe reasons we are interested in living and working in space. She would mention advantages and disadvantages of processing materials and manufacturing medicines and other items in space. She practiced demonstrations to show that oil and water or marshmallows and small hard candies mixed together in near-zero gravity do not separate as they would on earth. She would talk about important new products and knowledge that have resulted from our exploration of space. She planned to touch upon astronomy, earth observations, the communications satellite launched from *Challenger,* and the Spartan-Halley experiment to study Comet Halley.

Three experiments prepared by students who participated in the Shuttle Student Involvement Program (SSIP) would be on board *Challenger.* One was to observe the development of chicken embryos in space. Another would look at the effects of weightlessness on grain formation and strength in metals. The third student experiment used a semipermeable membrane to direct crystal growth.

As demonstrations for school viewing, Christa was to explain Newton's first, second, and third laws using a toy car and billiard balls as props. She would show students that even though mass has next to no weight in the near-zero gravity of space, a force is still needed to move it. Also, viewers would see that the more force applied to a mass, the faster it would accelerate. Christa planned to use billiard balls to show that for every action there is an equal and opposite reaction.

In the KC-135 training jet, Christa practiced an experiment about magnetism. During periods of weightlessness, small pieces of iron inside a clear plastic cube did not move directly toward an electromagnet at the center of the cube, as they would when affected by the earth's gravity. Instead, the bits of iron became arranged in a pattern along the magnet's fields of force.

Christa was to demonstrate simple machines such as the pulley and screw in space. On film she would show students interesting ways that pulleys are used in space. She would also try to remove a screw from a piece of wood with a screwdriver. Students would see that without her feet strapped in place only her body would turn, not the screw.

The most important experiment Christa planned to do in space was to grow bean sprouts without soil using liquid nutrients—a method known as hydroponics. Both the Soviet Union and the United States have grown plants in soil in space. But scientists have wondered whether plants could grow as well in space with only liquid nutrients.

Every day during flight Christa was to check the growth of six mung bean plants. One of the plants would be sprayed with a mist of nutrients. The other five plants would be growing directly in nutrient solution. At the same time, on earth, six plants would be grown under identical conditions, except for being earthbound. These plants later would be compared to those Christa would bring back from space.

From experiments like this astronauts may learn to grow vegetables in space station greenhouses to help supply some of their own food.

After the work was done on weightlessness training flights, it was time for fun. On one flight, Christa and Barbara Morgan played a gravity-free game of leapfrog, laughing all the while. Christa also tried folding her arms and doing a Russian cossack dance.

Part of Christa's training time was spent choosing the foods she would eat in space. NASA provided up to one hundred foods and forty-five beverages for her to taste. Then she designed her own menus. A computer checked the menus to be sure that they were nutritionally sound and that they provided three thousand calories per day.

Christa McAuliffe leapfrogs over Barbara Morgan during weightlessness training in the KC-135 training jet.

A typical dinner might include shrimp cocktail, beefsteak, rice pilaf, and broccoli au gratin. Dessert could be fruitcake, pudding, or cookies. Beverages could include cocoa, fruit drinks, lemonade, coffee, or tea. Snacks were much like those people eat at home: cashews, peanuts, graham crackers, granola bars, or candy.

Workers wearing surgical masks prepare space foods for the astronauts in NASA laboratories. Many of the foods are packaged in plastic pouches similar to the frozen foods in boilable pouches that people buy at the grocery store. Dehydrated, or dried, foods must have water added to soften the food. In space, water is injected into the packaged food in the orbiter's galley with a needle designed for this purpose. Other foods are irradiated or thermostabilized. These processes destroy bacteria in the foods that otherwise would cause them to spoil.

Space beverages come in square plastic containers. They are sipped through a straw. When the straw is not in use in space, a small plastic clamp must be placed on it to prevent liquid from escaping and floating freely about inside the living quarters.

Christa drinks from a space beverage container during simulator instruction.

Food for astronauts is usually put on board the space shuttle three days before flight. Because crew members design their own menus, they use color-coded food trays in space. Each astronaut is responsible for cleaning his or her own tray after eating.

Safety procedures were an important part of training. If an emergency made it necessary to abort a launch while the space shuttle was still on the pad, crew members would quickly exit the orbiter through the circular hatch in the left side. A catwalk would move into position so the crew could cross over to the towerlike service structure next to the space shuttle.

If one of *Challenger*'s main engines were to fail during the first few minutes after lift-off, the mission would be canceled. The spacecraft then would return to an emergency landing strip at the launch site in Florida or in Spain or Africa, depending upon when the engine failed. Before the landing, the solid rocket boosters and external fuel tank would separate from the orbiter. Then the orbiter could be piloted like an airplane back to earth.

Should an abnormal landing occur, Christa and the crew might need to jump from the circular hatch on the side of the orbiter. During training, Christa practiced swinging down from a bar on the open hatch door and dropping to the ground.

If a fire were to occur on the shuttle in orbit, smoke detectors would sound an alarm and a light on an instrument panel would come on to show the location of the fire. Each crew member would put on a portable oxygen system and then use a fire extinguisher to help put out the fire. During training, Christa put on a gas mask and air tank and doused a roaring fire to test her fire-fighting skills.

An extra supply of oxygen would be on board *Challenger* in case of a problem with the oxygen life-support system.

Challenger would have a medical kit with enough surgical equipment and medicines to sustain the crew. However, the most common ailment in flight is "space sickness," or nausea. It can last for a few hours or a few days. If necessary an astronaut could tape a wafer of medicine behind one ear. It would be absorbed slowly through the skin to ease the nausea.

Each of the space shuttle orbiters is equipped with two spacesuits. No extravehicular activities were planned for Mission 51-L. However, should another orbiter have to go into space to rescue *Challenger*'s crew, the commander and pilot of the stranded orbiter would each don a spacesuit. The other crew members would each be zipped into a personal rescue ball with a portable oxygen system. The rescue ball is made from the same materials as a spacesuit and is just large enough to hold a seated person. The commander and pilot then would be able to carry their fellow crew members to the refuge of the rescue orbiter.

If toxic fumes were to enter the orbiter's crew module, the spacesuits and rescue balls could be used to protect the astronauts. As soon as the crew members were in their personal rescue balls, the commander and pilot, in spacesuits, would depressurize the living quarters to vent the toxic gases into space. Then the crew module would be repressurized and the astronauts could safely remove their spacesuits or rescue balls.

Each astronaut would have a portable cassette player, earphones, and up to six tapes for entertainment. Each crew member also could bring up to twenty-four ounces of mementos or other personal items into space. Among the things Christa packed were her husband's class ring from the Virginia Military Institute, her daughter's cross and chain, her son's stuffed toy frog "Fleegle," a T-shirt with the New Hampshire state seal on it, a photograph of the student body at Marian High School with the school seal on it, a small hand-embroidered red-and-white pennant from Concord High School, and a T-shirt with one of her favorite mottoes on it: "I touch the future. I teach."

Throughout her training, Christa McAuliffe remained a teacher first. She called herself a space flight participant, not an astronaut. She worked hard and didn't hesitate to pitch in to

A copy of the photograph of the Marian High School student body that Christa took with her on the shuttle.

help others. The crew members admired her dedication. Near the time of launch, at a portrait session in Houston, the crew asked her to wait alone in a room for a few minutes. When they returned, they were wearing graduation caps with tassles and carrying school lunch boxes and apples!

NASA had limited Christa's time with the media to two hours a week during her training. Nevertheless, she managed to give interviews to every major U.S. newsmagazine, newspaper, and broadcasting network. She appeared on many popular television shows to answer questions about herself and the Teacher in Space Project. Her warmth, sincerity, and enthusiasm endeared her to the nation. She was the most celebrated astronaut since Sally Ride became the first American woman in space in June 1983.

4

Countdown to the Final Frontier

In November 1985 the space shuttle orbiter *Challenger* landed at Edwards Air Force Base in California after its ninth trip into space. From there it was flown piggyback on a Boeing 747 airplane to the Kennedy Space Center in Florida.

Ground crews in the Orbiter Processing Facility Building at the Kennedy Space Center inspected *Challenger* thoroughly. Its engines and its mechanical, electrical, and navigational systems were examined. Worn parts were replaced. More than thirty thousand insulating tiles, critical during the searing heat of reentry, were carefully checked for any defect.

Next, *Challenger* was rolled into the eight-acre, 525-foot-tall Vehicle Assembly Building. There huge cranes lifted the orbiter into an upright position to be joined to a new external fuel tank and two reusable solid fuel rocket boosters. When these procedures were completed, *Challenger* was ready to be moved to the launch pad.

A gigantic transporter-crawler—probably the largest land vehicle on earth—slowly inched the space shuttle toward Launch Pad 39B, approximately three miles away. The trip took several hours to complete. By December 30 *Challenger* was poised on the pad, aimed at the stars.

The original launch date for *Challenger* Mission 51-L was moved from Wednesday, January 22, to Saturday, January 25, because another shuttle, *Columbia,* returned later than scheduled from orbit. On Saturday a dust storm at one of the emergency landing strips halfway around the world, near Dakar, Senegal, in Africa, kept *Challenger* earthbound. NASA's safety rules would not allow a shuttle to be launched unless it had safe places to land should an emergency arise before it reached orbit. On Sunday, January 26, rain showers made launch impossible once again. Even a gentle rain could seriously damage the heat-resistant tiles of the orbiter because of the extraordinary speeds it would reach right after lift-off.

Monday dawned. At last the weather looked perfect for launch. After a breakfast of steak and eggs, Christa and her crewmates went to the "White Room" about ten stories above the launch pad. Here technicians in white coveralls vacuumed three times a day to keep everything dust-free. For days before the launch the seven astronauts had been kept in quarantine— away from people who might give them a cold or other communicable disease. Everything inside the orbiter *Challenger* and everyone entering it had to be perfectly clean. The technicians helped the astronauts put on their helmets and wiped each crew member's flight boots.

About two hours before the scheduled lift-off Christa and the crew crossed the catwalk to enter the circular hatch on the left side of *Challenger.* Technicians helped buckle them into their assigned seats, then left. The crew would lift off facing upward, lying on their backs.

The countdown reached T minus nine minutes. Then it was held there for four frustrating hours. The outside hatch handle of the orbiter could not be removed. A bolt that held the handle in place stubbornly refused to unscrew. During the delay the ideal weather conditions disappeared. The wind began gusting up to thirty-five miles per hour at the Kennedy Space Center. It would be too risky to land *Challenger* back at the Florida spaceport if the need to do so arose immediately after launch. For safety's sake, lift-off was scrubbed. Disappointed, Christa and the crew returned to isolation in their living quarters. The hatch door was replaced.

On Tuesday, January 28, *Challenger* glistened on the launch pad in the clear morning sky. The wind had slowed to nine miles per hour. During the night the temperature had fallen to 27°F. Before the crew went on board, a team of technicians was sent to check icicles on the shuttle and on the gantry, or support tower. The astronauts boarded *Challenger* and waited for launch as they had the previous day. Another ice inspection was made twenty minutes before scheduled lift-off. The ice did not appear to pose a threat to the heat tiles, so the countdown continued.

After days of delays, it looked as though *Challenger* would fly. Shivering spectators in bleachers began to cheer as the countdown clock advanced. Motorists in the area of the Kennedy Space Center, listening to the launch on their car radios, stopped alongside the highways and looked toward the ocean.

Teachers from all over the United States, including many of the Teacher in Space finalists, were on hand to watch Christa, one of their own, and the *Challenger* crew soar into space.

Crew members of Mission 51-L walk out of the Operations and Checkout Building on their way to Pad 39B to board *Challenger*.

Barbara Morgan, who had trained alongside Christa, stood on the top of a nearby building to get a good view. Christa's parents, sisters, and brothers watched from the VIP viewing stand. Scott McAuliffe's third-grade class was there as well.

Christa's husband and children stayed away from the crowded bleachers and watched from the top of another nearby building.

At T minus seven minutes thirty seconds, the catwalk was pulled away from the orbiter.

At T minus four minutes, Mission Control reminded the flight crew to close the airtight visors on their helmets.

At T minus forty-five seconds, the launch platform was flooded with water to lessen the deafening roar of lift-off and to prevent damage to the spacecraft.

At T minus twenty-five seconds, the main engine firing sequence was turned over to the on-board computers.

When the countdown reached T minus ten seconds, everyone in the viewing stands—relatives, teachers, school children, dignitaries, and friends—began to chant along.

Nine . . . eight . . . seven . . .

At T minus six seconds, the main engines fired. Flames spewed forth.

Five . . . four . . . three . . . two . . . one.

The solid rocket boosters ignited.

Lift-off!

Within seven seconds, *Challenger* had cleared the tower of Launch Pad 39B.

Elation—a mixture of pride, patriotism, and pure joy—swept through the spectators at the Kennedy Space Center, the teachers and students watching on monitors in classrooms, and the viewers in front of television sets throughout America. For one beautiful minute a nation stood in awe, and the wonder of space exploration lived again.

Then, without warning, at 11:39 A.M. a cloud of billowing smoke and orange fire filled the sky. Barely seventy-four seconds into flight, the space shuttle exploded. Before the nation's eyes, *Challenger* and its heroic crew were lost.

For everyone, elation and joy instantly turned to unspeakable horror and grief. Resounding cheers became stunned silence.

Americans had witnessed the worst tragedy in the history of space flight.

This photograph, taken about sixty seconds after launch, shows an unusual plume of flame in the lower part of the right solid rocket booster.

5

Triumph From Tragedy

Following the explosion of *Challenger* the whole nation grieved at the death of seven space heroes. Everywhere, flags flew at half-staff. Americans had not been so deeply touched by a tragedy since the assassination of President John F. Kennedy in 1963. Every citizen was moved by the loss. President Reagan, members of Congress, former astronauts, teachers, students, and people from every corner of the country and all walks of life expressed their deep sense of sorrow.

President Ronald Reagan immediately sent Vice-President George Bush to the Kennedy Space Center to offer condolences to the families of the astronauts. The president was to deliver his State of the Union address the evening of January 28. Instead, he postponed it for one week and gave a speech that afternoon from the Oval Office in tribute to the *Challenger* astronauts.

He told the families of the seven, "Your loved ones were daring and brave and they had that special grace, that special spirit that says, 'Give me a challenge and I'll meet it with joy.' They had hunger to explore the universe and discover its truths. They wished to serve and they did—they served all of us."

Flags fly at half-mast in the nation's capital the day following the *Challenger* tragedy.

And to the schoolchildren who were watching, President Reagan said, "I know it's hard to understand that sometimes painful things like this happen. It's all part of the process of exploration and discovery, it's all part of taking a chance and expanding man's horizons. The future doesn't belong to the fainthearted. It belongs to the brave. The *Challenger* crew was pulling us into the future and we'll continue to follow them."

President Reagan closed his speech by saying, "We will never forget them nor the last time we saw them this morning as they prepared for their journey and waved goodbye and 'slipped the surly bonds of earth to touch the face of God.'"

On January 30 Christa's alma mater, Framingham State College, held a memorial service attended by about a thousand people. Included were Christa's parents and other family members. Governor Michael Dukakis of Massachusetts and other dignitaries paid tribute to Christa McAuliffe and the *Challenger* astronauts. Christa's former professor of history, A. Carolla Haglund, recalled that Christa had taken her course, "The American Frontier." It was about women pioneers and their diaries of life on the frontier. Christa had told Professor Haglund that the course changed her life.

Following the service, hundreds of students met outside the auditorium to sing "America" and to release a bouquet of seven black balloons symbolizing the *Challenger* astronauts.

The next day, January 31, President Reagan honored the *Challenger* heroes at a service at the Johnson Space Center in Houston, where they had trained. It was broadcast nationwide. Relatives of the astronauts and thousands of NASA employees attended. The president first met privately with the relatives.

Later, in the eulogy, he said of the seven astronauts, "We will always remember them, these skilled professionals . . . and we will cherish each of their stories—stories of triumph and bravery, stories of true American heroes."

President Reagan spoke for all Americans when he said, "The sacrifice of your loved ones has stirred the soul of our nation and, through the pain, our hearts have been opened to a profound truth: the future is not free, the story of all human progress in one of a struggle against all odds. We learned again that this America . . . was built by men and women like our seven star voyagers, who answered a call beyond duty, who gave more than was expected or required, and who gave it with little thought to worldly reward."

The president continued, "Sometimes when we reach for the stars, we fall short. But we must pick ourselves up again and press on. . . . Today we promise Dick Scobee and his crew that their dream lives on. . . . Man will continue his conquest of space, to reach out for new goals and ever greater achievements. That is the way we shall commemorate our seven *Challenger* heroes."

After President Reagan spoke, the band played "God Bless America" and NASA T-38 jets thundered overhead in the traditional "missing man" formation that symbolized the loss of a pilot.

President Reagan shook hands somberly and offered condolences to Christa McAuliffe's husband and parents and other
relatives of the *Challenger* astronauts. Both he and Mrs. Reagan
gave hugs and words of comfort to the astronauts' children who
attended.

There were many other tributes to Christa McAuliffe and
the *Challenger* crew. Students at Concord High School, where
Christa had taught, held a memorial assembly the same day as
the ceremonies in Houston. The president of the student council
read a two-page letter from President Reagan. It described
Christa as "a woman of courage and caring, an educator of
boundless energy and inexhaustible enthusiasm, an inspiration
to young and old alike."

In Concord, New Hampshire, the hometown Christa had
described as a "Norman Rockwell" kind of place, people
gathered on the State House plaza on the night of January 31.
They were bundled against the bitter cold in mittens, scarfs, and
heavy coats to pay tribute to their friend, neighbor, and teacher,
Christa McAuliffe. Dignitaries drew lessons from her life and
death. They spoke of how she would be a role model for young
people for generations to come. Only one month before, many
of these same people had come to this plaza to celebrate New
Year's Eve and to watch Christa judge a snow sculpture contest
with the theme "Reach for the Stars." Now seven bells tolled
solemnly from the tower of St. Paul's Church in memory of the
seven astronauts.

A service was held at the Kennedy Space Center in Florida
on February 1. NASA employees there wanted to pay their
respects to the *Challenger* astronauts. A large wreath of white
carnations was dropped from a helicopter into the ocean where
debris from the destroyed space shuttle had rained into the
water.

Two days later, a private funeral mass was attended by Christa McAuliffe's family at St. Peter's Church in Concord, New Hampshire. Friends came as well, including Barbara Morgan, the alternate for the Teacher in Space mission.

A nationwide flag-raising ceremony was coordinated by the Kentucky Department of Education. On February 4, at 11:39 A.M., exactly one week after *Challenger* exploded, education officials at sites in over thirty states raised the flag of "learning and liberty," a special flag to commemorate the importance of public education. Christa had carried two hundred small versions of the flag with her and was to distribute them after the flight.

Many states also have started scholarship funds in Christa McAuliffe's memory to help students who want to become teachers. In New Hampshire, at a ceremony on February 7, Governor John Sununu announced the formation of a "living memorial" trust fund. Every year it will allow one New Hampshire teacher a year-long leave from the classroom to explore studies outside his or her field. The program will keep alive the meaning of Christa's mission by promoting the love of knowledge and spirit of discovery in dedicated teachers. The fund has been approved by members of Christa's family who attended the announcement. A family member will help direct the fund. The first representative to do so will be Christa's mother.

At the first full session of the House of Representatives in New Hampshire, the members stood silent in honor of Christa McAuliffe and her lost crewmates.

One of Christa McAuliffe's goals in life was to increase public appreciation and respect for teachers. Another was to get students involved in the space program. She had succeeded mightily before the ill-fated flight of *Challenger*. However, since the disaster, an extraordinary outpouring of tributes has been made to honor Christa McAuliffe and benefit members of her profession or students who want to become teachers.

Representative Gary Ackerman of New York introduced legislation in the U.S. House of Representatives in Washington to designate January 28, the day of the tragedy, National Teachers' Recognition Day.

William Bennett, U.S. secretary of education, has announced that one million dollars will be used to provide 340 Christa McAuliffe Scholarships. These will enable teachers from any field to study with leading scholars in science and mathematics during the summer of 1987.

Both the National Education Association and the American Federation of Teachers have announced scholarship funds in Christa McAuliffe's name. These will provide grants to teachers who wish to explore their subjects in new or innovative ways.

Classroom Earth is a nonprofit group that planned to help with the broadcasts of the lessons from space. They will raise money in Christa's name to give seven annual scholarships. One scholarship will be given in each of the professions practiced by the *Challenger* astronauts. The group is asking students who would have watched the lessons from space to give twenty-five cents to the scholarship fund.

Foreign governments sent messages of sympathy to the astronauts' relatives and the American people. The Japanese minister of science and technology was so moved after attending the memorial service in Houston that he wanted to do something for Concord High School as a tribute to Christa McAuliffe. He returned to Japan and won the support of Prime

Minister Nakasone, Japanese cabinet ministers, and an organization of Japanese businesses to donate to a $100,000 fund for the high school.

Many students have responded to the loss of *Challenger* and its crew by donating money to build a new space shuttle. One program is called "Pennies for Space—Rebuild the Spirit." It was started by high school students in Bath, New York. A nine- and ten-year-old sister and brother in Gillette, Wyoming, are raising money for a new shuttle. They have asked every American child to donate one dollar. A thirteen-year-old student in Grants Pass, Oregon, is raising funds for a new shuttle as well. Children at the Camel's Hump School in Richmond, Vermont, have begun collecting pennies to help pay for future shuttle flights.

In addition, a nonprofit scientific and educational group, the United States Space Foundation of Colorado Springs, Colorado, is raising money for a new shuttle. The foundation itself has donated $10,000. One company in Colorado that manufactures rocket fuel has pledged 2 percent of its profits to the foundation over the next two years. The total could reach $250,000.

NASA has estimated that a new space shuttle would cost about two billion dollars—an enormous sum. NASA can accept donations, but by law, the administration cannot earmark the funds for a specific use. A lawyer for the United States Space Foundation is working with people from NASA to see if this obstacle can be overcome, however.

Other tributes continue. In Washington, D.C., the American Security Bank established a trust fund for the eleven children of the *Challenger* astronauts. In the first week after the disaster, the bank had received more than fifty-one hundred contributions.

When all of the tributes to Christa McAuliffe and the *Challenger* crew have been made, what will be the future of the space program? Representative William Nelson of Florida had flown on the previous shuttle mission only a few weeks before the tragedy. Despite the great loss, he has emphasized the importance of the space program. America's ability to compete in international markets depends on new technology and discoveries made in space. He asserted: "Let's find the problem, let's correct it, and let's get on with the program."

There were several theories of what caused the explosion of the space shuttle on January 28. However, the strongest suspicions centered on one of the solid rocket boosters. When films of the space shuttle's lift-off and climb skyward were viewed, an unusual plume of flame could be seen coming from the area near a joint on the lower part of the right solid rocket booster.

On February 3, President Reagan named a presidential commission to investigate the cause of the *Challenger* disaster. It was headed by former secretary of state William P. Rogers. Neil A. Armstrong, the first astronaut to step onto the moon, and Sally K. Ride, the first American woman into space, were members, along with other prominent space experts and engineers.

After an extensive sea search, much of the debris from the disaster was found, including large sections of *Challenger* and the rocket boosters. Remains of the astronauts were also recovered, and each family decided on a final ceremony. Christa was buried in her hometown in New Hampshire on May 1, 1986.

Our nation depends heavily on the space shuttle program. Expensive satellites in orbit will need to be repaired by people. Other satellites wait to be launched into orbit. Many industries in the United States want to do research and manufacturing in space. What has been learned in space has been used to improve products used by all of us. NASA has planned to transport the future space station into orbit section by section in the shuttle's cargo bay for assembly in space.

Many other important payloads have been planned for future shuttle missions. An example of only one of these is the Hubble Space Telescope. This telescope was to be put into orbit by the shuttle in 1986. High above the veil of the earth's atmosphere, it will expand man's view into deep space. To astronomers, the Space Telescope is one of the most dramatic advances since the invention of the telescope in 1610. They hope to learn more about the origins of the universe than has been known up to now.

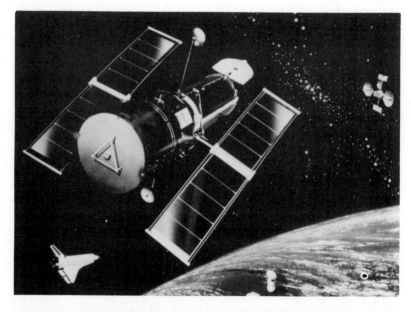

The Hubble Space Telescope is forty-three feet long and weighs more than 25,000 pounds. After it is launched, it will operate 320 miles above the Earth.

Administrators at NASA said that when the space shuttles will fly again, a teacher would be the next civilian passenger. Barbara Morgan, who trained alongside Christa McAuliffe as a backup, accepted NASA's offer to be the next teacher in space. She said, "We have the opportunity to teach an entire generation a very important lesson. The *Challenger*'s mission was the schoolchildren's mission. Their whole orientation to space and to life depends on what happens next. . . . They think of themselves as our partners in space exploration. I am ready to be their partner."

The Young Astronaut program was established by President Reagan to encourage young people in the United States to study space-related sciences and mathematics. Thousands of Young Astronaut chapters have been started. Each one is headed by a teacher or a leader from the community. The Young Astronaut Council in Washington, D.C., distributes a curriculum to the chapters that covers mathematics, engineering, physics, computers, and other areas of science. They provide activities that are fun and that teach. A monthly newsletter is sent to chapter heads.

Some Young Astronaut members have established ties with Young Cosmonauts in Russia in an effort to promote peace through space.

Since the tragedy of *Challenger,* "Space exploration ironically has been given an extraordinary lift among young people throughout America," said the executive director of the Young Astronaut Council, Wendell Butler.

Though she did not give her well-practiced lessons from space, Christa McAuliffe fulfilled her goals as the teacher in space. Americans have a renewed appreciation and respect for the teaching profession. There has been a rebirth of interest and the sense of wonder in America's space program. Nowhere is this more evident than among schoolchildren in classrooms across the United States. To them, Christa McAuliffe was the ultimate teacher. They sent thousands of letters and drawings to her family in Concord, New Hampshire, and to the students and faculty at the high school where Christa taught.

Perhaps this adaptation of a line from *The Education of Henry Adams* describes Christa McAuliffe's legacy best: "A teacher affects eternity; no one can tell where her influence stops." For each of us who was touched by teacher Christa McAuliffe's shining example of commitment and courage, her primary lesson will always live. We must press onward to meet the challenges of the future. We must bravely follow our dreams and "reach for the stars." To do less would fall short of the honor we owe to Christa McAuliffe and her fellow *Challenger* astronauts who flew for all of us.

One of the tributes to Christa McAuliffe made by students.

Index